one bowl meals

COOKBOOK

DEVELOPED BY

WILLIAMS SONOMA

TEST KITCHEN

Photographs Annabelle Breakey

weldon**owen**

Contents

Mediterranean Chicken Salad Bowl with
Bulgur & Tapenade Dressing (page 25)

Spiralized Vegetable Bowl with
Crispy Quinoa & Pistachios (page 38)

Great Bowls of Fun

Everyone loves to eat from bowls. They're friendly and welcoming—and just plain fun. Filled with uncomplicated and delicious food, bowl dishes pack a lot of punch into one single-serving vessel. Simple yet balanced, these recipes are your road map to quicker, easier, and healthier meals. What's more, these complete feasts are practical, designed for everyday enjoyment and even eating on the go.

Within these pages, you'll discover the many benefits of bowls. They're versatile—easy to eat solo yet bountiful enough to share with guests. The ingredient options are endless and full of variety, so you'll be able to cook with whatever you have on hand, making weeknight dinners and breakfasts on frenzied mornings a snap.

In the 27 recipes that follow, you'll find a bowl for every occasion. A colorful and nutritious Acai Bowl with Mango, Kiwifruits, Raspberries, Goji Berries & Chia Seeds (page 54) is the perfect way to start the day. Pack a filling and energizing Spiralized Vegetable Bowl with Crispy Quinoa & Pistachios (page 38) for lunch, and then tuck into a cozy bowl of Short-Rib Bibimbap with Kimchi-Zucchini Slaw & Fried Egg (page 31) for dinner. You'll even find deconstructed versions of some of your favorite non-bowl recipes, like the mouthwatering Pork Belly Banh Mi Bowl (page 15). There's truly something for every palate, preference, and mood. Once you learn how easy it is to layer textures, colors, and flavors, there's no doubt that you'll become a bowl pro.

All About Ingredients

We eat with our eyes, so it's no surprise that an aesthetically beautiful bowl is even more delightful to enjoy. From the nourishing grain or noodle base to the array of veggies and meats that cover it, each ingredient has an important role to play. This is food you can feel good about, with their many health benefits wrapped up into a pretty package.

COLOR IS KEY Don't be shy about adding lots of colorful fruits and vegetables when they are fresh and in season. Bowls are an easy way to eat the rainbow.

DO DOUBLE DUTY Protein-packed quinoa and good-for-your-gut kimchi are just two examples of foods that provide both a tasty and a nutritious element to your feast.

PREP AHEAD Cook grains in big batches to use all week, and mix sauces separately so they're easily packable and portable for lunch. Many dressings (like creamy avocado or tangy lemon za'atar yogurt) can be used for a variety of dishes, so keep your favorites in the fridge to speed up prep at mealtime. All of the dressing recipes (pages 56–58) will last up to 1 week in the refrigerator.

THE MORE THE MERRIER Many of these meals are easily served family style by doubling the quantities of each ingredient, or set up a bar and let everyone assemble their own bowl.

Which bowl to use?

Of course, bowl preferences are so personal. We love a wide, shallow bowl, which lets you see all of the bounty that you are about to enjoy, while a deep bowl lets you slowly uncover the goodies that await. We're a fan of digging in with a traditional fork or even opting for a spoon, spork (spoon-fork hybrid), or chopsticks.

Thai Chicken Bowl with Green Beans,
Eggplant & Coconut Rice (page 48)

Chipotle Chicken Bowl with Butternut
Squash & Charred Corn (page 26)

Building Your Bowl

The key to a nourishing and satisfying bowl lies in how you build it. Focusing on the right mix of contrasting textures (soft, smooth, crispy, crunchy) with complementary flavors creates the best results. You can't miss with this formula for the perfect bowl. The possibilities are endless!

BUILD YOUR BASE Pick a hearty base (see ideas at right) that will add fiber and carbs to your bowl and also soak up all the lovely juices from your dressing or marinade. There's an option for everyone, whether you're wanting to eat gluten-free, lower your carb count, or increase your fiber intake.

ADD PROTEIN Arguably the star of a bowl, protein lends texture, flavor, and heft. Use top-quality ingredients and don't be afraid of a little fat, which adds huge flavor. Try omega-filled salmon, nuts and beans, tofu, skin-on chicken, or grass-fed beef.

TOP IT UP Load up your bowl with lots of fresh, nutritious toppings, including vegetables, fruits, and seeds. The bigger the variety in texture and flavor, the more enticing your bowl will be. Aim for a balance of crunchy toppings, such as kimchi, pickles, carrots, or radishes, and soft toppings, like avocado, eggs, mushrooms, or arugula. Also, think about how each element is prepared and aim for a variety of cooked and raw ingredients, as well as ones that are cut into different shapes and sizes.

FINISH IT OFF Condiments and dressings add flavor, richness, and salt to a bowl and bind it together to make a meal. A sprinkling of crumbly cheese, a handful of olives, a few crostini, or a dollop of hummus are delicious ways to complete a bowl. Try the flavor-packed dressings (pages 56–58), or to streamline prep, use store-bought salsa, tzatziki, or a favorite jarred sauce to finish off your bowl.

What can be used for the base of your bowl?

These hearty grains and vegetables make the perfect base for a nutritious meal.

- Barley
- Bulgur
- Farro
- Polenta or grits
- Quinoa
- Oatmeal
- Rice (brown, white, or wild)
- Noodles (rice or wheat)
- Roasted root vegetables
- Spiralized raw vegetables
- Salad greens

Chickpea Fritters

WITH ROASTED CARROTS, CABBAGE SALAD & PITA CHIPS

A varied combination of flavors, textures, and colors, this Middle Eastern–influenced bowl is a nutritional powerhouse, with a rich lode of vitamins, minerals, protein, and fiber. You can assemble and shape the fritters a day in advance and keep them refrigerated until just before frying.

To make the chickpea fritters, in a food processor, combine the garlic and onion and pulse until chopped. Add the chickpeas, corn, parsley, cilantro, 2 teaspoons salt, the cumin, and red pepper flakes and process until blended. Add the flour and baking powder and process until just combined. Transfer the chickpea batter to a bowl, cover, and refrigerate until thoroughly chilled, about 3 hours.

Meanwhile, make the pita chips, cucumber-tomato salad, cabbage salad, and roasted carrots. Set all aside until ready to serve.

To fry the chickpea fritters, in a large, deep frying pan, pour in canola oil to a depth of 2 inches and heat until it reaches 325°F on a deep-frying thermometer. Using an ice-cream scoop or 2 spoons and working in batches, shape the batter into 2-inch balls and drop them, one at a time, into the hot oil. Fry until crispy and cooked through, about 2 minutes per side. Using a slotted spoon or a spider, transfer the fritters to a paper towel–lined plate and sprinkle with salt.

Divide the cabbage salad among 4–6 bowls. Top with the chickpea fritters, cucumber-tomato salad, roasted carrots, pita chips, and hummus. Garnish with parsley and serve.

serves 4—6

FOR THE CHICKPEA FRITTERS

3 cloves garlic

1 small yellow onion, roughly chopped

1 can (15 oz) chickpeas, drained and rinsed

1 cup fresh corn kernels (from about 2 ears)

3 tablespoons chopped fresh flat-leaf parsley

2 tablespoons chopped fresh cilantro

Kosher salt

1½ teaspoons ground cumin

1 teaspoon red pepper flakes

7 tablespoons all-purpose flour

1 teaspoon baking powder

1 recipe Pita Chips (page 60)

1 recipe Cucumber-Tomato Salad (page 59)

1 recipe Cabbage Salad (page 59)

1 recipe Roasted Carrots (page 59)

Canola oil, for frying

Kosher salt

1 cup hummus

Chopped fresh flat-leaf parsley, for garnish

For a portable bowl, pack the salads and fritters into the hollow of a pita bread and top with a spoonful of hummus.

To enhance the flavor of the sesame toasts, warm the sesame oil with a few tablespoons of chopped lemongrass for 1 minute, then remove it before adding the bread.

Pork Belly Bahn Mi Bowl

WITH PICKLED CARROTS & DAIKON, CILANTRO, JALAPEÑO & SESAME CRISPS

Rice noodles can replace the rice in this deconstructed version of the popular Vietnamese sandwich: cook 12 oz dried noodles in boiling water according to package directions, drain, rinse with cold water, and toss with a little sesame oil.

To make the pork belly, preheat the oven to 375°F. Season the pork with salt. In a Dutch oven over medium-high heat, warm the oil. Add the pork, skin side down, and cook until browned on both sides, about 3 minutes per side. Transfer to a plate. Reduce the heat to medium, add the shallots, and cook, stirring occasionally, until softened, about 3 minutes. Add the garlic and ginger and cook, stirring occasionally, until lightly browned and fragrant, about 1 minute. Add the soy sauce, maple syrup, and fish sauce and stir to combine. Remove from the heat. Return the pork, skin side up, to the pot. Add enough water to almost cover the pork, leaving about ¼ inch exposed. Bake until the skin is crispy and darkened and the meat is very tender, 2–2½ hours.

Make the picked carrots, jasmine rice, sesame toasts, and maple glaze. Set all aside until ready to serve.

In a small bowl, combine the mayonnaise and Sriracha and stir until blended. In a medium bowl, toss together the cucumbers and the 1 tablespoon oil and season with salt.

Transfer the pork to a cutting board, let it rest for 5 minutes, then cut it into thin slices. Divide the rice evenly among 4 bowls. Top with the pork, picked carrots, sesame toasts, Sriracha mayonnaise, cucumbers, jalapeño, radishes, and cilantro, if using. Drizzle with the maple glaze and serve.

serves 4

FOR THE PORK BELLY

1½ lb skin-on, center-cut pork belly, cut in half

Kosher salt

3 tablespoons sesame oil

2 shallots, diced

3 cloves garlic, grated

1 tablespoon peeled and grated fresh ginger

3 tablespoons soy sauce

3 tablespoons maple syrup

2 tablespoons Asian fish sauce

1 recipe Pickled Carrots (page 60)

1 recipe Jasmine Rice (page 58)

1 recipe Sesame Toasts (page 61)

1 recipe Maple Glaze (page 57)

½ cup mayonnaise

2 teaspoons Sriracha chili sauce

2 cucumbers, halved lengthwise and sliced

1 tablespoon toasted sesame oil

1 jalapeño chile, sliced

4 radishes, thinly sliced

Fresh cilantro leaves, for garnish (optional)

Teriyaki Salmon Bowl

WITH CUCUMBERS, GRILLED PINEAPPLE, ZUCCHINI & AVOCADO

Begin this meal with a bowl of miso soup, punctuated with diced tofu and strips of seaweed, and finish it with green tea ice cream accompanied by sesame or almond cookies. Pour hot tea or cold beer at the table.

In a bowl, whisk together the sake, sesame oil, and soy sauce. Add the cucumbers and toss to coat. Let stand for at least 15 minutes.

Heat a grill pan over medium-high heat and brush with canola oil. Working in batches, grill the pineapple and zucchini until tender-crisp and charred, about 3 minutes per side. Transfer to a cutting board and let cool slightly. Cut the pineapple into 1-inch cubes and the zucchini into ½-inch half-moons. Keep warm.

To make the teriyaki sauce, in a small saucepan over high heat, combine the soy sauce, mirin, sake, and brown sugar and bring to a boil. Reduce the heat to medium and simmer until thickened, about 3 minutes.

Brush half of the teriyaki sauce over the salmon. In a large sauté pan over medium-high heat, warm the canola oil. Add the salmon and sear until cooked through, about 4 minutes per side. The flesh should be opaque and flaky and easily pierced with a paring knife. Remove from the heat and brush with the remaining teriyaki sauce.

Divide the rice among 4 bowls. Drain the cucumbers and distibute them evenly among the bowls. Top with the pineapple, zucchini, salmon, and avocado. Garnish with sesame seeds. Drizzle with soy sauce and serve.

serves 4

½ cup sake

3 tablespoons sesame oil

1 tablespoon soy sauce

2 cucumbers, thinly shaved

Canola oil for brushing

1 pineapple, peeled and cut into planks about 1 inch thick

2 zucchini, halved lengthwise

FOR THE TERIYAKI SAUCE

¼ cup soy sauce

¼ cup mirin

2 tablespoons sake

2 tablespoons firmly packed light brown sugar

1½ lb salmon fillets, cut into 4 equal pieces

1 tablespoon canola oil

Steamed sushi rice, for serving

2 avocados, pitted, peeled, and thinly sliced

White sesame seeds, for garnish

Soy sauce, for drizzling

To add a crispy texture
to the fish, use skin-on
salmon fillets and sear
the skin side first.

Cut into a kefta to see if it's cooked through. If not, reduce the heat to low, cover, and cook for about 5 minutes longer.

Lamb Kefta Bowl

WITH CUCUMBER SALAD, TOMATOES, BELL PEPPERS & CHILI OIL

To grill the kefta, shape the meatballs around metal or bamboo skewers, then grill on an oiled rack over a medium-high fire, turning as needed. Slide off the skewers to serve. Lamb and yogurt is a classic combination. A drizzle of chili oil adds nuance.

Make the toasted flatbread and the cucumber salad. Set both aside until ready to serve.

To make the lamb kefta, in a sauté pan over medium heat, warm 2 tablespoons of the oil. Add the onion and cook, stirring occasionally, until tender, about 4 minutes. Add the garlic and cook, stirring occasionally, until fragrant, about 1 minute. Transfer to a large bowl and let cool. Stir in the parsley, chopped cilantro, cumin, fennel, coriander, red pepper flakes, and 1 teaspoon salt. Add the lamb and gently mix until blended. Divide into 12–16 equal pieces and form into football-shaped meatballs.

In a large sauté pan over medium heat, warm the remaining 2 tablespoons oil. Working in batches if needed, cook the kefta until browned on all sides and cooked through, 12–14 minutes total. Keep warm.

In a small frying pan over low heat, warm the ⅓ cup oil and the chili powder until sizzling, about 3 minutes. Pour all but about 1 tablespoon of the oil into a bowl and set aside for serving. Warm the remaining oil in the pan over medium-high heat. Add the tomatoes and bell peppers and cook, stirring often, until the tomatoes are blistered and the peppers are tender, about 4 minutes. Remove from the heat and stir in the cilantro leaves. Season with salt and pepper. Divide the tomato mixture and cucumber salad among 4 bowls.

Place 3–4 meatballs and a few strips of flatbread in each bowl and top evenly with the yogurt. Drizzle with the reserved chili oil and serve.

serves 4

1 recipe Toasted Flatbread (page 61)

1 recipe Cucumber Salad (page 59)

FOR THE LAMB KEFTA

4 tablespoons olive oil

1 yellow onion, minced

3 cloves garlic, minced

½ cup fresh flat-leaf parsley leaves, chopped

½ cup fresh cilantro leaves, chopped

1 teaspoon ground cumin

1 teaspoon ground fennel

1 teaspoon ground coriander

1 teaspoon red pepper flakes

Kosher salt

1½ lb ground lamb

⅓ cup olive oil

1 tablespoon chili powder

2 cups cherry tomatoes

2 green bell peppers, seeded and diced

1 cup fresh cilantro leaves

Kosher salt and freshly ground black pepper

¼ cup plain Greek yogurt

Curried Chicken Salad Bowl

WITH SHREDDED CARROT SALAD, ENDIVE & PITA

A satisfying lunch or light dinner, this chicken salad surprises with crisp shards of pita among the finely cut vegetables. To save time on serving day, toast the pita up to 3 days in advance and store it in an airtight container at room temperature.

Preheat the oven to 350°F.

Place the pita rounds on a baking sheet. Bake until toasted and crispy, about 5 minutes. Let cool, then tear into bite-size pieces. Set aside.

Put the chicken in a large saucepan, add water to cover, and bring to a boil over high heat. Reduce the heat to medium and poach until the chicken is cooked through, about 20 minutes. Drain and let cool to room temperature. Cut the meat into 1-inch cubes.

In a large bowl, stir together the mayonnaise, vinegar, 1 tablespoon of the mustard, and the curry powder. Stir in the green onions, raisins, cashews, and celery. Add the chicken and toss to coat. Season with salt and pepper.

In another large bowl, whisk together the shallot, lemon zest and juice, and the remaining 1 tablespoon mustard. Slowly whisk in the oil. Season with salt and pepper. Add the carrots, parsley, and pita bread and toss to coat.

Divide the carrot salad among 4 bowls. Top with the chicken salad and garnish with the green onion tops. Divide the endive leaves among the bowls to use as a scoop for the chicken salad. Serve right away, or cover and refrigerate for up to 3 days.

serves 4

2 pita rounds

2 lb skinless, boneless chicken breasts

1½ cups mayonnaise

2 tablespoons champagne vinegar

2 tablespoons Dijon mustard

3 tablespoons curry powder

3 green onions, white and pale green parts, thinly sliced, dark green tops reserved for garnish

¼ cup raisins

½ cup chopped roasted cashews

2 ribs celery, finely diced

Kosher salt and freshly ground pepper

2 tablespoons minced shallot

Zest and juice of 1 lemon

⅓ cup olive oil

4 carrots (about ½ lb total weight), peeled and shredded

½ cup fresh flat-leaf parsley leaves

2 heads Belgian endive, leaves separated

Harissa Shrimp & Grits Bowl

WITH KALE & PRESERVED LEMON

If you do not have fiery hot North African harissa paste on hand, substitute Korean gochujang, Indonesian sambal ulek, or your favorite thick Chinese or Thai garlic-chili paste, adjusting the amount according to your palate and the intensity of the paste.

In a saucepan over high heat, bring 3 cups water to a boil. Slowly whisk in the grits and a pinch each of salt and pepper. Reduce the heat to medium-low and cook, stirring occasionally, until thickened, about 5 minutes. Stir in the cheese, butter, and crème fraîche. Remove from the heat and adjust the seasoning with salt and pepper. Cover to keep warm.

In a wide, deep frying pan over medium heat, warm 2 tablespoons of the oil. Add the onion and cook, stirring occasionally, until soft and translucent, about 4 minutes. Raise the heat to medium-high and add the kale. Cook, stirring occasionally, until wilted, about 10 minutes. Stir in the preserved lemon and season with salt and pepper. Set aside.

Pat the shrimp dry and place in a bowl. Add 2 tablespoons of the oil and the harissa paste and toss to coat. Heat a grill pan or a large frying pan over medium-high heat. Grill or sauté the shrimp until opaque throughout, 2–3 minutes per side. Transfer to a plate.

In a large sauté pan over medium-high heat, warm the remaining 1 tablespoon oil. Add the tomatoes and cook, stirring occasionally, until blistered and starting to pop, about 3 minutes. Season with salt.

Divide the grits, kale, shrimp, and tomatoes among 4 bowls. Top with a dollop of crème fraîche and serve.

serves 4

¾ cup instant grits

Kosher salt and freshly ground pepper

¼ cup grated Parmesan cheese

2 tablespoons unsalted butter

2 tablespoons crème fraîche, plus more for serving

5 tablespoons olive oil

1 small yellow onion, diced

2 bunches kale, thick stems removed, leaves thinly sliced

1 preserved lemon, seeded, flesh and peel diced

1½ lb large shrimp, peeled and deveined, with tails intact

3 tablespoons harissa paste

2 cups cherry tomatoes

Grilled Steak Bowl

WITH CHARRED CORN, PICKLED SHALLOTS & CHIMICHURRI

If your butcher doesn't carry flank steak, skirt, flatiron, or hanger steak will work equally well here. A crumbly, pungent blue cheese is a good substitute for the feta, and a small red onion can replace the shallots.

Make the chimichurri; set aside.

½ cup Chimichurri (page 57)

To make the pickled shallots, put the shallots in a heatproof bowl. In a small saucepan over medium-high heat, combine ½ cup water, the vinegar, sugar, 1 tablespoon salt, the peppercorns, and bay leaf. Bring to a simmer, stirring until the sugar and salt are dissolved. Pour over the shallots, making sure they are completely submerged, and let cool. Use right away, or transfer the shallots and their liquid to an airtight container and refrigerate for up to 1 week.

FOR THE PICKLED SHALLOTS

2 shallots, sliced ¼ inch thick

½ cup red wine vinegar

¼ cup sugar

Kosher salt

4 peppercorns

1 bay leaf

Heat a grill pan over high heat. Cook the corn until evenly charred, about 8 minutes total. When the corn is cool enough to handle, cut the kernels from the cobs. Set aside.

4 ears corn, husks and silks removed

1 lb flank steak

Season the steak with salt and pepper. Brush the pan with the oil. Grill the steak until cooked to your liking, about 4 minutes per side for medium-rare. Transfer to a cutting board, cover loosely with aluminum foil, and let rest for 5 minutes.

Kosher salt and freshly ground pepper

1 tablespoon canola oil

Zest and juice of 1 lemon

In a small bowl, whisk together the lemon zest and juice, vinegar, and olive oil. Season with salt and pepper. Put the arugula in a bowl, drizzle with the vinaigrette, and toss. Add the cheese and corn and toss again.

1 tablespoon champagne vinegar

¼ cup olive oil

½ lb arugula

¼ lb feta cheese, crumbled

Divide the arugula salad among 4 bowls. Thinly slice the steak across the grain and add to the bowls. Drizzle with the chimichurri, top with the pickled shallots, and serve.

serves 4

For another layer of flavor and even more protein, toss some cooked quinoa into the arugula salad.

Instead of thinly slicing the cucumber, you can make ribbons by running a vegetable peeler lengthwise along the cucumber, creating paper-thin strips. Discard the seedy center.

Mediterranean Chicken Salad Bowl

WITH BULGUR & TAPENADE DRESSING

In good weather, season the chicken as directed, then cook it on an outdoor grill for a delicious smoky, charred flavor. If you like, trade out the hummus for a yogurt-herb dip and the feta for semifirm halloumi cheese.

Make the tapenade dressing; set aside.

To make the bulgur salad, cook the bulgur according to the package instructions. Let cool slightly, then stir in the lemon zest and juice, parsley, and oil, and season with salt and pepper. Set aside.

Season the chicken generously with salt and pepper. In a large frying pan over medium-high heat, warm the oil. Working in batches, add the chicken and cook until opaque throughout, about 5 minutes per side, adding more oil to the pan if the chicken begins to stick. Transfer the chicken to a cutting board and cut into slices. Set aside.

Divide the bulgur salad among 4 bowls. Top with the onion. Peel and thinly slice the cucumber, layering it over the onion. Halve the tomatoes, layering them over the cucumber. Add the cheese, olives, chicken, and hummus to each bowl. Garnish with the parsley, drizzle with the tapenade dressing, and serve.

serves 4

1 recipe Tapenade Dressing (page 57)

FOR THE BULGUR SALAD

1½ cups bulgur

1 teaspoon grated lemon zest

1 tablespoon fresh lemon juice

1 cup loosely packed fresh flat-leaf parsley leaves, finely chopped

3 tablespoons olive oil

Kosher salt and freshly ground pepper

6 skinless, boneless chicken thighs (about 1 lbs total weight)

Kosher salt and freshly ground pepper

3 tablespoons olive oil, plus more as needed

1 red onion, diced

1 cucumber

2 cups cherry tomatoes

½ lb feta cheese, sliced

1 cup pitted Kalamata olives

1 cup hummus

Fresh flat-leaf parsley leaves, for garnish

Chipotle Chicken Bowl

WITH BUTTERNUT SQUASH & CHARRED CORN

Make this substantial chicken bowl in the early fall, when corn and winter squash are both at the market. To change up the combination here, use Sugar Pie pumpkin or Red Kuri squash for the butternut squash and pinto beans for the black beans.

Make the avocado dressing; set aside.

Place 1 rack in the upper third and 1 rack in the lower third of the oven. Preheat the oven to 375°F. In a bowl, mix the butternut squash and pearl onions with 2 tablespoons of the oil, and season with salt and pepper. Spread in a single layer on a baking sheet. Roast on the upper rack until easily pierced with a knife, about 30 minutes.

Meanwhile, in another bowl, stir together the chipotle chiles, cumin, and a pinch *each* of salt and pepper. Add the chicken and toss to coat. Transfer to a baking sheet. Roast on the lower rack until an instant-read thermometer inserted into the thickest part of a thigh, away from the bone, registers 165°F, about 25 minutes.

Heat a grill pan over high heat. Cook the corn until evenly charred, about 8 minutes total. When the corn is cool enough to handle, cut the kernels from the cobs. Set aside.

In a large sauté pan over medium-high heat, warm the remaining 1 tablespoon oil. Add the beans and cook, stirring occasionally, until warmed through, about 2 minutes. Add the tomatoes, green onions, and cilantro and toss until the tomatoes are slightly blistered, about 2 minutes.

Divide the avocado dressing among 4 bowls. Top with the bean mixture, squash and onions mixture, corn, and chicken. Garnish with radishes, cilantro, and sour cream and serve.

serves 4

1 recipe Avocado Dressing (page 56)

1 butternut squash (about 2 lbs), peeled and cut into 1-inch cubes

½ lb pearl onions, peeled and halved

3 tablespoons olive oil

Kosher salt and freshly ground pepper

2 chipotle chiles in adobo sauce, roughly chopped

1 teaspoon ground cumin

4 skin-on, bone-in chicken thighs (about 2 lb total weight)

2 ears of corn, husks and silk removed

1 can (15 oz) black beans, drained and rinsed

2 cups cherry tomatoes

2 green onions, white and pale green parts, thinly sliced

½ cup loosely packed fresh cilantro leaves, roughly chopped

Radishes, fresh cilantro, and sour cream, for serving

For a heartier meal, serve atop a bed of Spanish Rice (page 58) or steamed white or brown rice mixed with a sprinkling of chopped fresh cilantro.

Sweet Potato Hash

WITH POACHED EGG & CHIMICHURRI

Cut down on cleanup time by cooking the eggs on the hash: cook the hash as directed, make 4 shallow indentations in the surface, crack an egg into each one, and then bake in a preheated 400°F oven until the whites have set but the yolks are still slightly runny, about 10 minutes.

Make the chimichurri; set aside.

Bring a large pot of water to a boil over high heat. Add 1 teaspoon salt and the sweet potatoes and cook until fork-tender, 10–12 minutes. Drain and set aside.

In a large cast-iron skillet over medium-high heat, cook the pancetta, stirring occasionally, until crispy, about 8 minutes. Using a slotted spoon, transfer the pancetta to a paper towel–lined plate. Add the onion and bell peppers to the skillet and cook, stirring occasionally, until tender, about 4 minutes. Add the garlic and cook, stirring occasionally, for 1 minute. Season with salt and pepper. Transfer the onion and peppers to the plate with the pancetta and set aside.

In the same skillet over medium-high heat, warm ¼ cup of the oil. Add the sweet potatoes and cook without stirring until crispy and browned underneath, 7–10 minutes. Flip the potatoes and cook until crispy and browned on the other side, 7–10 minutes longer. Add the reserved pancetta, onions and peppers, and the remaining ¼ cup oil. Cook, stirring occasionally, until the vegetables are warmed through and the potatoes are crispier, about 10 minutes. Season with salt and pepper.

Just before serving, make the poached eggs. Divide the hash among 4 bowls. Top with the poached eggs and season with salt and pepper. Drizzle with the chimichurri and serve.

serves 4

1 recipe Chimichurri (page 57)

Kosher salt and freshly ground pepper

2½ lb sweet potatoes, peeled and cut into 1-inch cubes

½ lb pancetta, cut into 1-inch pieces

1 yellow onion, diced

2 red bell peppers, seeded and cut into 1-inch pieces

3 cloves garlic, minced

½ cup olive oil

4 poached eggs (page 61)

Lox Bowl

WITH FARRO, GRAPEFRUIT SALAD & PICKLES

Smoked trout fillet makes an excellent substitute for the lox here, pairing well with the salad, citrus, and pickles, and pearled barley (cooked according to package instructions) is a good stand-in for the farro. If you prefer a sweeter flavor, choose red grapefruit over yellow.

Make the lemon za'atar yogurt; set aside.

Bring a large pot of salted water to a boil over high heat. Add the farro and cook until tender but still a bit chewy, 25–30 minutes. Drain and transfer to a bowl. Add the lemon juice and 2 tablespoons of the oil and toss to coat. Set aside.

Using a sharp knife, carefully cut away the peel and pith from each grapefruit, then cut the fruit into rounds about ¼ inch thick. Place in a bowl and add the onion, watercress, and half of the dill. Add the remaining 2 tablespoons oil and the vinegar and toss to combine. Season with salt and pepper.

Divide the farro and the grapefruit salad among 4 bowls and top with the lox. Garnish with the remaining dill. Top with the pickles, cornichons, and a dollop of the lemon za'atar yogurt and serve.

serves 4

1 recipe Lemon Za'atar Yogurt (page 57)

Kosher salt and freshly ground pepper

1 cup farro, rinsed

Juice of 1 lemon

4 tablespoons olive oil

2 grapefruits

½ red onion, thinly sliced

2 cups watercress or arugula

¼ cup fresh dill fronds

1 tablespoon white wine vinegar

½ lb lox or smoked salmon

1 cup bread and butter pickles

1 cup cornichons

Kimchi is a traditional Korean side dish made with fermented seasoned vegetables. It can be purchased online, in Asian markets, and in many grocery stores.

Short-Rib Bibimbap

WITH KIMCHI-ZUCCHINI SLAW & FRIED EGG

Bibimbap, literally "mixed rice," is a classic Korean dish consisting of rice with a variety of toppings. Gochujang—a Korean condiment made from red chiles, glutinous rice, and fermented soybeans—adds pungent flavor.

To prepare the short ribs, in a large bowl, whisk together the soy sauce, sesame oil, garlic, brown sugar, and sesame seeds. Add the short ribs and toss to coat. Let stand at room temperature for 30 minutes, or cover and refrigerate up to overnight.

In a large nonstick frying pan over medium-high heat, warm the sesame oil. Add the rice and pack it down in an even layer. Cook without stirring until the rice browns and crisps, about 10 minutes, rotating the pan and adjusting the heat as needed to prevent burning. Transfer to a bowl; set aside.

Wipe out the pan if necessary, then warm the canola oil over medium heat. Add the garlic and ginger and cook, stirring frequently, until crisp and brown, about 3 minutes. Using a slotted spoon, transfer the garlic and ginger to a paper towel–lined plate and set aside. Add the spinach to the pan and cook, stirring frequently, until wilted, about 3 minutes. Transfer the spinach to a bowl, season with salt, and set aside. Make the kimchi-zucchini slaw; set aside.

Heat a grill pan over medium-high heat. Place the short ribs on the pan and cook until browned on both sides, about 3 minutes per side. Transfer to a cutting board, cover loosely with aluminum foil, and let rest for 5 minutes. Cut into slices between the bones, or trim off the line of bones and then slice the meat across the grain.

To serve, divide the rice among 4 bowls. Top each with short ribs, spinach, kimchi-zucchini slaw, and a fried egg. Garnish with the garlic and ginger. Serve gochujang alongside.

serves 4

FOR THE SHORT RIBS

2 tablespoons soy sauce

1 tablespoon sesame oil

2 cloves garlic, minced

2 teaspoons firmly packed light brown sugar

1 teaspoon sesame seeds

1 lb short ribs, cut across the bone into ½-inch slices (flanken or Korean style)

1 tablespoon sesame oil

3 cups steamed short-grain rice

2 tablespoons canola oil

2 tablespoons minced garlic

1 tablespoon peeled and minced fresh ginger

10 oz baby spinach leaves

Kosher salt

1 recipe Kimchi-Zucchini Slaw (page 59)

4 fried eggs (page 61)

Gochujang, for serving

Chipotle Lime Shrimp Bowl

WITH SPANISH RICE & ROASTED RADISHES

You can make the dressing and bake the tortilla strips the day before serving this flavor-filled bowl, packing each into an airtight container and storing the dressing in the refrigerator and the strips at room temperature.

Make the cilantro dressing, tortilla strips, Spanish rice, and lime crema; set aside. Preheat the oven to 425°F.

To make the shrimp, in a medium bowl, whisk together the chipotle chiles, oil, lime zest and juice, honey, and ¼ teaspoon salt. Pat the shrimp dry, add them to the bowl, and toss to coat. Let stand at room temperature for 15 minutes.

Meanwhile, make the roasted radishes: In a small bowl, toss together the radishes and oil, and season with salt and pepper. Spread, cut side down, in a single layer on a baking sheet. Roast until the radishes begin to brown but are still firm inside, 8–10 minutes. Transfer to a small bowl. Add the cilantro and 3 tablespoons of the cilantro dressing and toss to coat.

Heat a large nonstick frying pan over medium-high heat. Place the shrimp in a single layer in the pan and cook until opaque throughout, about 2-3 minutes per side.

Divide the Spanish rice among 4 bowls. Top with the shrimp, radishes, tortilla strips, and avocado. Garnish with a dollop of lime crema, drizzle with the remaining cilantro dressing, and serve with the lime wedges.

serves 4

1 recipe Cilantro Dressing
(page 56)

1 recipe Tortilla Strips
(page 61)

1 recipe Spanish Rice
(page 58)

1 recipe Lime Crema
(page 58)

FOR THE SHRIMP

2 chipotle chiles in adobo
sauce, minced

1 tablespoon canola oil

1 teaspoon grated lime zest

1 tablespoon fresh lime juice

1 teaspoon honey

Kosher salt

1 lb medium shrimp, peeled
and deveined

FOR THE ROASTED
RADISHES

1 bunch radishes, trimmed
and halved

1 tablespoon canola oil

Kosher salt and freshly
ground pepper

2 tablespoons minced fresh
cilantro

1 avocado, pitted, peeled,
and sliced

Lime wedges, for serving

Chicken is a good alternative to the shrimp in this flavorful bowl. Use diced boneless chicken breast, and cook as directed for the shrimp.

Sausage & Polenta Bowl

WITH KALE, MUSHROOMS & SUN-DRIED TOMATO PESTO

You can skip the pesto or use store-bought and this Italian-inspired bowl will still be delicious. If you cannot find semolina polenta (coarse-ground hard wheat), substitute the more common corn-based polenta, and cook it over medium heat, stirring often, for about 30 minutes.

Make the sun-dried tomato pesto; set aside.

To make the sausage and vegetables, in a large frying pan over medium-high heat, cook the sausage, crumbling it with a wooden spoon, until browned and cooked through, about 10 minutes. Using a slotted spoon, transfer the sausage to a paper towel–lined plate, cover with aluminum foil, and keep warm until ready to serve.

In the same pan over medium heat, cook the onion, stirring occasionally, until translucent and slightly charred, about 10 minutes. Add the garlic and cook, stirring occasionally, for 1 minute. Add the kale and cook, stirring occasionally, until tender, about 5 minutes. Set aside.

In another large frying pan over medium-high heat, warm the oil. Add the mushrooms and cook, stirring occasionally, until tender, 6–8 minutes. Season with salt and pepper. Set aside.

To make the polenta, in a large saucepan over medium heat, bring the milk to a vigorous simmer. Remove from the heat, add the polenta, and whisk constantly until the polenta has thickened, about 2 minutes. Stir in the cheese and rosemary, and season with salt and pepper.

Divide the polenta among 4 bowls. Top with the sausage, kale, mushrooms, and pesto. Garnish with cheese and pine nuts and serve.

serves 4

1 recipe Sun-Dried Tomato Pesto (page 56)

FOR THE SAUSAGE & VEGETABLES

1 lb mild Italian sausage, casing removed

1 large yellow onion, diced

3 cloves garlic, minced

1 bunch kale, thick stems removed, leaves roughly chopped

¼ cup olive oil

1 lb shiitake mushrooms, brushed clean and sliced

Kosher salt and freshly ground pepper

FOR THE POLENTA

4¾ cups milk

1½ cups semolina polenta

¼ cup grated Parmesan cheese

2 tablespoons minced fresh rosemary

Kosher salt and freshly ground pepper

Grated Parmesan cheese and toasted pine nuts, for serving

Barley & Chickpea Bowl

WITH MUSHROOMS, KALE & RADISH-ASPARAGUS SALAD

Fleshy-stemmed, buttery-tasting king trumpet mushrooms (aka king oyster or French horn) contribute a meat-like quality to this vegetarian bowl, but they can be hard to find. Abalone or oyster mushrooms, which are close relatives, cremini, or matsutake mushrooms can be substituted.

Make the lemon za'atar yogurt, radish-asparagus salad, and crispy spiced chickpeas; set aside.

To make the barley, in a large saucepan over medium-high heat, warm the oil. Add the barley and cook, stirring often, until fragrant, about 2 minutes. Add the broth and ½ teaspoon salt. Raise the heat to high and bring to a boil. Reduce the heat to low, cover, and simmer until the barley is tender yet still maintains a bite, about 25 minutes. Drain off any excess liquid. Season with salt and pepper. Set aside.

Meanwhile, make the kale: in a large sauté pan over medium heat, warm the oil and garlic until the garlic begins to brown, about 2 minutes. Add the kale and toss to coat. Cover and cook until the kale is just tender, about 5 minutes. Uncover and cook until any liquid evaporates. Transfer the kale to a plate. Season with salt and lemon juice. Remove and discard the garlic clove.

To make the mushrooms, in the same pan over medium-high heat, warm the oil. Add the mushrooms and cook, stirring occasionally, until tender and browned, about 6 minutes, adding the garlic during the last 2 minutes of cooking. Transfer the mushrooms to a plate. Season with salt.

Divide the barley among 4 bowls. Top with the chickpeas, kale, mushrooms, radish-asparagus salad, and a generous spoonful of the lemon za'atar yogurt.

serves 4

1 recipe Lemon Za'atar Yogurt (page 57)

1 recipe Radish-Asparagus Salad (page 59)

1 recipe Crispy Spiced Chickpeas (page 60)

FOR THE BARLEY

1 tablespoon olive oil

1 cup pearl barley

2½ cups vegetable broth

Kosher salt and freshly ground black pepper

FOR THE KALE

1 tablespoon olive oil

1 clove garlic, smashed

1 bunch kale, thick stems removed, leaves roughly chopped

Kosher salt

Fresh lemon juice, to taste

FOR THE MUSHROOMS

1 tablespoon olive oil

½ lb king trumpet, cremini, or matsutaki mushrooms, brushed clean and sliced

1 clove garlic, minced

Kosher salt

If you prefer tuna cooked to medium, increase their time over the heat—searing them about 2 minutes longer per side.

Seared Tuna Bowl

WITH RICE NOODLES, MANGO & SPICY MAYO

When choosing mangoes for this bowl, look for plump, oval fruits that give slightly to the touch and have a sweet, fruity aroma. The sunny yellow Ataulfo variety has particularly creamy flesh. Offer room-temperature cooked spinach, tossed with soy sauce and toasted sesame oil, on the side.

Make the avocado dressing; set aside.

In a small bowl, stir together the mayonnaise and Sriracha. Set aside.

Cook the rice noodles according to the package instructions. Drain, transfer to a bowl, add the avocado dressing, and toss to coat. Divide the noodles among 4 bowls and sprinkle with the green onions.

In a wide, shallow bowl, stir together the white and black sesame seeds. Press the edges of each tuna steak into the sesame seeds to coat. In a large sauté pan over medium-high heat, warm the oil. Sear the tuna on the sesame seed–coated sides until the seeds are crispy and the tuna is opaque on the edges, 1–2 minutes per side. Top each bowl with a tuna steak.

In a bowl, toss together the mangoes and chili powder and divide among the bowls. Top with the spicy mayo, pickled ginger, and nori and serve.

serves 4

1 recipe Avocado Dressing (page 56)

½ cup mayonnaise

1 tablespoon Sriracha chili sauce or chili garlic paste

½ lb rice noodles

4 green onions, dark green parts only, thinly sliced

¼ cup white sesame seeds

¼ cup black sesame seeds

1½ lb good-quality ahi tuna, cut into 4 equal pieces

2 tablespoons canola oil

2 mangoes, pitted, peeled, and cut into ½-inch cubes

½ teaspoon chili powder

¼ cup pickled ginger

1 sheet nori, thinly sliced

Spiralized Vegetable Bowl

WITH CRISPY QUINOA & PISTACHIOS

An easy-to-use, inexpensive kitchen tool, the spiralizer quickly turns nearly any firm vegetable into noodle-like ribbons. If you don't have one, you can still make this recipe, using a sharp knife and a steady hand to cut the vegetables into thin, fine julienne.

Make the green goddess dressing; set aside.

Spiralize the zucchini, radishes, beets, carrots, and fennel using the shredder blade of a spiralizer, stopping to cut the strands every 3–4 rotations. Place each spiralized vegetable in a separate bowl. Season each with a squeeze of lemon juice and a pinch of salt.

Heat a nonstick frying pan over medium-high heat. Toast the quinoa, stirring frequently, until it begins to brown and smell nutty, about 8 minutes. The quinoa will crackle and pop as it toasts. Transfer to a small bowl.

In the same pan over medium heat, toast the pistachios, stirring frequently, until lightly browned and fragrant, about 3 minutes. Transfer to another small bowl.

Divide the green goddess dressing among 4 bowls. Arrange the spiralized vegetables in the bowls. Top with the quinoa and pistachios and serve.

serves 4

1 recipe Green Goddess Dressing (page 56)

2 zucchini, ends trimmed

5 radishes, ends trimmed

4 beets (about 6 oz total weight), peeled and ends trimmed

3 carrots, peeled and ends trimmed

1 fennel bulb, ends trimmed

1 lemon

Kosher salt

½ cup quinoa, rinsed

½ cup raw pistachios

Toasted quinoa adds
pleasant crunch and
unique flavor to a fresh
and colorful blend of
spiralized raw vegetables.

If the duck still needs to be cooked after the initial searing, roast in a 400°F oven, checking every 5 minutes, until done.

Korean BBQ Duck Bowl

WITH CILANTRO-SESAME SLAW, SNAP PEAS & RICE

To give this Korean-inspired duck bowl a little chile heat, add 1–2 tablespoons of Korean red chile paste (gochujang) to the marinade. Cilantro-infused cabbage adds tender crunch and fresh flavor.

Make the cilantro dressing; set aside.

In a bowl, whisk together the soy sauce, vinegar, sesame oil, garlic, green onions, brown sugar, ginger, and ½ teaspoon pepper. Add the duck, cover, and refrigerate for at least 1 hour or up to overnight. Let stand at room temperature for 30 minutes before cooking.

Heat a grill pan or large sauté pan over medium-high heat and brush with canola oil. Remove the duck from the marinade, reserving the marinade. Place the duck, skin side down, in the pan and cook until charred on both sides and an instant-read thermometer inserted into the thickest part of the duck, away from the bone, registers 165°F, about 8 minutes per side. Transfer the duck to a cutting board, cover loosely with aluminum foil, and let rest for 5 minutes.

In a large bowl, toss together the cabbage, cilantro, and cilantro dressing. Season with salt and pepper and sprinkle with the sesame seeds; set aside.

In a large sauté pan over high heat, simmer the reserved marinade until slightly thickened, about 3 minutes. Stir in the snap peas and cook until tender-crisp, about 3 minutes.

Divide the brown rice among 4 bowls. Top with the snap peas and sauce, and the cilantro-sesame slaw. Thinly slice the duck and divide among the bowls. Garnish with green onions and ginger and serve.

serves 4

1 recipe Cilantro Dressing (page 56)

¼ cup soy sauce

2 tablespoons rice vinegar

2 tablespoons toasted sesame oil

3 cloves garlic, grated

2 green onions, white and pale green parts, sliced

1 tablespoon firmly packed light brown sugar

2 teaspoons peeled and grated fresh ginger

Kosher salt and freshly ground pepper

2 lb skin-on, bone-in duck breasts

Canola oil, for brushing

½ head green cabbage, cored and thinly shredded

½ cup loosely packed fresh cilantro leaves, roughly chopped

3 tablespoons white sesame seeds

½ lb sugar snap peas, trimmed and sliced

Steamed brown rice, for serving

Thinly sliced green onions and julienned fresh ginger, for garnish

Five-Spice Steak Bowl

WITH RICE VERMICELLI, CARROT-CUCUMBER SALAD & CRISPY SHALLOT

A cast-iron grill pan brushed with lemongrass-infused oil offers subtle seasoning to spiced flank steak in this Asian-inspired bowl. Shaved carrots and cucumbers add color, crispness, and fresh flavor.

Make the crispy shallot; set aside.

In a small frying pan over medium-low heat, warm the oil. Add the lemongrass and cook, stirring occasionally, until fragrant and tender, about 5 minutes. Strain the oil and discard the lemongrass. Set aside.

In a large bowl, stir together the ¼ cup lime juice, the fish sauce, vinegar, brown sugar, and garlic. Cook the rice noodles according to the package instructions. Drain, transfer to the bowl, and toss to coat.

Sprinkle the steak with the five-spice powder and a pinch *each* of salt and pepper. Let stand at room temperature for 30 minutes. Heat a grill pan over high heat and brush with the lemongrass-scented oil. Grill the steak until cooked to your liking, about 5 minutes per side for medium-rare. Transfer to a cutting board, cover loosely with aluminum foil, and let rest for 5 minutes.

In a bowl, toss together the carrots, cucumber, mint, and the juice of 1 lime, and season with salt and pepper.

Divide the noodles among 4 bowls. Top with the carrot-cucumber salad and the bean sprouts. Thinly slice the steak across the grain, divide among the bowls, and top with the crispy shallot. Garnish with jalapeño, lime wedges, and mint leaves and serve.

serves 4

1 recipe Crispy Shallot (page 60)

2 tablespoons canola oil

2 lemongrass stalks, white and pale green parts, thinly sliced

¼ cup fresh lime juice plus juice of 1 lime

¼ cup Asian fish sauce

¼ cup rice vinegar

¼ cup firmly packed light brown sugar

2 cloves garlic, grated

½ lb rice vermicelli or other thin rice noodles

1½ lb flank steak

2 teaspoons Chinese five-spice powder

Kosher salt and freshly ground pepper

2 carrots, peeled and thinly shaved

1 cucumber, thinly shaved

1 cup fresh mint leaves

1 cup bean sprouts

Thinly sliced jalapeño chile, lime wedges, and mint leaves, for garnish

Farro & Pea Salad Bowl

WITH GOAT CHEESE

The curly tendrils and tiny leaves of pea shoots look especially attractive atop this bowl, but if your market does not have them, young, tender watercress sprigs can be used in their place. Feta or a mild blue can be substituted for the goat cheese.

Make the green goddess dressing; set aside.

Bring a large pot of salted water to a boil over high heat. Add the farro and cook until tender but still a bit chewy, 25–30 minutes. Drain and transfer to a large bowl. Add the the ¼ cup oil and the lemon zest, and season with salt and pepper. Stir in the peas and mint. Let cool.

In a small bowl, toss together the pea shoots, lemon juice, and 2 teaspoons oil. Set aside.

Fill a large saucepan three-fourths full of lightly salted water and bring to a boil over high heat. Add the snap peas and cook until tender, about 3 minutes. Drain, rinse with cold water, and pat dry. Cut the snap peas on the bias into ½-inch pieces.

Divide the green goddess dressing among 4 bowls. Top with the farro mixture, pea shoots, snap peas, pistachios, and goat cheese. Serve with lemon wedges.

serves 4

1 recipe Green Goddess Dressing (page 56)

2 cups farro, rinsed

¼ cup plus 2 teaspoons olive oil

1 tablespoon grated lemon zest

Kosher salt and freshly ground pepper

1½ cups fresh or thawed frozen peas

1 cup fresh mint leaves, thinly sliced

2 cups pea shoots

2 teaspoons fresh lemon juice

2 cups sugar snap peas, trimmed

1 cup pistachios, toasted

½ lb goat cheese, crumbled

Lemon wedges, for serving

Soba Noodle Bowl

WITH ASPARAGUS, SHIITAKES, EGG & KIMCHI

When asparagus is out of season, use 1 lb green beans in their place, adjusting the blanching and browning times as needed to achieve a crisp-tender result. For a more showy garnish, top with an equal amount of white and black sesame seeds.

To make the soba noodles, in a medium bowl, whisk together the tahini, lime juice, soy sauce, honey, oil, garlic, and 3 tablespoons water. Season with salt and pepper. Set aside. Cook the soba noodles according to the package instructions. Drain, transfer to a large bowl, and set aside.

To make the vegetables, in a large frying pan over medium-high heat, warm 2 tablespoons of the oil. Add the asparagus and cook, stirring occasionally, until browned, about 7 minutes. Add 1 tablespoon of the soy sauce and cook for 1 minute longer. Transfer to a plate and cover loosely with aluminum foil.

In the same pan over medium-high heat, warm another 2 tablespoons of the oil. Add the bok choy and cook, stirring occasionally, until browned, about 5 minutes. Add the remaining 1 tablespoon soy sauce and cook for 1 minute longer. Transfer to a plate and cover loosely with foil.

In the same pan over medium-high heat, warm the remaining 2 tablespoons oil. Add the mushrooms and cook, stirring occasionally, until browned and tender, about 6-8 minutes. Season with salt. Set aside.

Prepare the medium-boiled eggs. Peel and halve lengthwise.

Add the tahini dressing to the noodles, thinning the dressing with 1–2 tablespoons of water if needed. Toss the noodles to coat, and divide among 4 bowls. Top with the vegetables, eggs, and kimchi. Garnish with the green onions and sesame seeds and serve.

serves 4

FOR THE SOBA NOODLES

1½ cups tahini

3 tablespoons fresh lime juice

2 tablespoons soy sauce

2 tablespoons honey

2 tablespoons toasted sesame oil

2 cloves garlic, minced

Kosher salt and freshly ground pepper

10 oz dried soba noodles

FOR THE VEGETABLES

6 tablespoons sesame oil

1 bunch (about 1 lb) asparagus, trimmed and cut into 3-inch pieces

2 tablespoons soy sauce

2 heads bok choy, leaves separated, cut into 3-inch pieces

1½ lb shiitake mushrooms, brushed clean, stemmed, and sliced

Kosher salt

1 recipe medium-boiled eggs (page 61)

1 cup kimchi

½ cup sliced green onions

3 tablespoons sesame seeds

For a wheat-free option in this vegetarian bowl, use thick or thin rice noodles in place of the soba.

Extract as much liquid
as possible from the
tofu before cooking it to
achieve the best golden
and crispy crust.

Crispy Tofu Bowl

WITH BROCCOLINI, EDAMAME & PEANUT SAUCE

If broccolini is not available, you can still make this healthy bowl. Just turn to either of the two vegetables—broccoli or Chinese broccoli—that went into creating the popular brassica hybrid, trimming them so you have small florets on slender stems.

Make the peanut sauce; set aside.

Drain the tofu, wrap it in paper towels, place a heavy plate on top, and let stand for 10 minutes to press out the excess liquid. Cut the tofu into 1-inch cubes.

In a large sauté pan over medium heat, warm the oil. Working in batches if needed, add the tofu cubes and cook until crispy and golden on all sides, about 2 minutes per side. Using a slotted spoon, transfer to a paper towel–lined plate.

In the same pan over medium-high heat, cook the shallots and broccolini, stirring often, until tender-crisp, about 6 minutes. Add the bell peppers and cook, stirring often, until all the vegetables are tender, about 4 minutes. Stir in the edamame and soy sauce and cook until the edamame are warmed through, about 1 minute.

Divide the rice among 4 bowls and top with the tofu and vegetables. Drizzle with the peanut sauce, garnish with the green onions and peanuts, and serve.

serves 4

1 cup Peanut Sauce (page 58)

2 lb firm tofu

½ cup canola oil

2 shallots, thinly sliced

1 lb broccolini, bottoms trimmed

2 red bell peppers, seeded and thinly sliced

1 cup frozen edamame, thawed

1 tablespoon soy sauce

Steamed white rice, for serving

2 green onions, white and pale green parts, thinly sliced

¼ cup roasted peanuts, crushed

Thai Chicken Bowl

WITH GREEN BEANS, EGGPLANT & COCONUT RICE

For a lighter preparation, omit the coconut milk and increase the water to 3¾ cups for cooking the rice. Expand the garnish by adding julienned cucumber and small cilantro sprigs with the chiles and green onions.

To make the chicken, in a large bowl, whisk together the soy sauce, oil, brown sugar, ginger, and garlic. Add the chicken and stir to coat. Cover and refrigerate for 30 minutes.

Make the coconut rice. Cover and set aside.

Preheat the oven to 375°F. Remove the chicken from the marinade, discarding the marinade, and place on a baking sheet. Roast until the skin is caramelized, about 40 minutes. Transfer to a cutting board and let cool. Remove the meat from the bones and cut into strips. Set aside.

To prepare the vegetables, in a large frying pan over medium-high heat, warm the oil. Add the green beans in a single layer and cook without stirring until blistered, about 4 minutes. Flip the green beans and cook 4 minutes longer. Add the soy sauce and cook 1 minute. Using a slotted spoon, transfer the beans to a plate and cover with foil.

Add the eggplants to the pan and cook, stirring often, until most of the oil has been absorbed, about 3 minutes. Raise the heat to high, add the ginger and garlic, and cook, stirring often, until the eggplants are tender and the ginger and garlic are browned and crisp, about 8 minutes. Stir in the brown sugar and fish sauce, if using. Transfer the eggplant mixture to a separate plate and cover with foil. Add the chiles to the pan and cook, stirring occasionally, until lightly charred and tender, about 5 minutes.

Divide the rice among 4 bowls. Top with the chicken, eggplant mixture, and green beans. Garnish with the chiles and green onions. Serve with lime wedges.

serves 4

FOR THE CHICKEN

½ cup soy sauce

2 tablespoons sesame oil

1 tablespoon firmly packed light brown sugar

2 teaspoons peeled and grated fresh ginger

2 cloves garlic, minced

6 skin-on, bone-in chicken thighs (about 2½ lb total)

1 recipe Coconut Rice (page 58)

FOR THE VEGETABLES

¼ cup sesame oil

10 oz green beans, trimmed

2 teaspoons soy sauce

2 Asian eggplants, cut into 3-inch strips

3-inch piece fresh ginger, peeled and thinly sliced

2 cloves garlic

1 teaspoon light brown sugar

2 teaspoons Asian fish sauce (optional)

2 red chiles, sliced

Thinly sliced green onions, for garnish

Lime wedges, for serving

For a bigger hit of coconut flavor, add ½ teaspoon coconut extract to the rice along with the coconut milk and water.

This deconstructed fresh spring roll contains all the essential components of the popular Southeast Asian dish.

Spring Roll Bowl

WITH RICE NOODLES & PEANUT SAUCE

If you have peanut-sensitive diners at your table, omit the peanut sauce and chopped nuts and top each bowl with a simple soy-based sauce: season soy sauce to taste with chili-garlic sauce, a little honey, sliced green onions, and toasted white sesame seeds.

Make the peanut sauce; set aside.

In a large frying pan over medium-high heat, pour in oil to a depth of ½ inch and heat until hot but not smoking. Add the wonton wrappers and fry until golden brown and crisp, about 1 minute per side. Using a slotted spoon, transfer the wonton wrappers to a plate and sprinkle with salt. Set aside.

In a large sauté pan over medium-high heat, warm the 2 tablespoons oil. Add the mushrooms, garlic, and ginger and cook, stirring occasionally, until the mushrooms are tender, about 6–8 minutes. Add the soy sauce, toss to coat, and cook 1 minute longer. Keep warm.

Cook the rice noodles according to the package instructions. Drain, transfer to a bowl, add the vinegar, and toss to coat.

Divide the noodles among 4 bowls and top with the mushrooms, lettuce, mint, basil, carrots, and cucumber. Garnish with the wonton wrappers and peanuts. Drizzle with the peanut sauce and serve.

serves 4

1 cup Peanut Sauce (page 58)

Canola oil for frying, plus 2 tablespoons

8 wonton wrappers

Kosher salt

½ lb shiitake mushrooms, brushed clean, stemmed, and roughly chopped

2 cloves garlic, minced

2-inch piece fresh ginger, peeled and minced

1 tablespoon soy sauce

½ lb rice noodles

2 tablespoons rice vinegar

1 head romaine lettuce, shredded

½ cup fresh mint leaves, thinly sliced

½ cup fresh basil leaves, thinly sliced

2 carrots, peeled and thinly sliced

1 cucumber, thinly sliced

½ cup chopped peanuts

Savory Oatmeal

WITH ROASTED CHERRY TOMATOES, PESTO, POACHED EGG, AVOCADO & CHIVES

Here is the ideal bowl for a casual Saturday brunch. Transfer the leftover pesto to a jar, top with a thin layer of olive oil, cap tightly, and refrigerate for up to a week, then use to dress up pasta or sandwiches.

Preheat the oven to 400°F.

To make the oatmeal, in a large saucepan over medium-high heat, melt the butter. Add the oats and cook, stirring frequently, until golden and fragrant, about 2 minutes. Add the broth and ½ teaspoon kosher salt and bring to a boil. Reduce the heat to low, cover, and simmer until the oats are just tender, about 20 minutes.

Meanwhile, make the roasted tomatoes: In a bowl, toss together the tomatoes, oil, vinegar, and a pinch *each* of salt and pepper. Spread in a single layer on a baking sheet. Roast until the tomatoes are blistered and beginning to burst, 18–20 minutes. Set aside.

Make the pesto; set aside.

Divide the oatmeal among 4 bowls. Top with the tomatoes, avocado, feta, a spoonful of the pesto, and the poached eggs. Sprinkle with the chives, flaked sea salt, and pepper and serve.

serves 4

FOR THE OATMEAL

1 tablespoon unsalted butter

1 cup steel-cut oats

3 cups vegetable broth

Kosher salt

FOR THE ROASTED CHERRY TOMATOES

2 cups cherry tomatoes

1 tablespoon olive oil

1 teaspoon balsamic vinegar

Kosher salt and freshly ground pepper

1 recipe Basil-Arugula Pesto (page 56)

1 avocado, pitted, peeled, and sliced

½ cup crumbled feta cheese

1 recipe poached eggs (page 61)

¼ cup minced fresh chives

Flaked sea salt and freshly ground pepper

Coconut Quinoa Porridge

WITH TOASTED COCONUT FLAKES, RASPBERRIES, BANANA & PISTACHIOS

Although white quinoa is called for here, you can also make this hearty breakfast bowl with red or black quinoa, for a more boldly colored—and slightly crunchier—porridge. If using black quinoa, increase the cooking time by about 5 minutes.

In a saucepan over high heat, combine the quinoa, coconut milk, vanilla, cinnamon, and a pinch of salt and bring to a boil. Reduce the heat to low, cover, and cook until most of the liquid has been absorbed and the quinoa is tender, 13–15 minutes. Remove from the heat and stir in the maple syrup.

Divide the porridge between 2 bowls. Top with the coconut flakes, pistachios, almond butter, banana, and raspberries. Serve right away.

serves 2

1 cup white quinoa, rinsed

1 can (13.5 fl oz) coconut milk

½ teaspoon pure vanilla extract

½ teaspoon ground cinnamon

Kosher salt

2 tablespoons pure maple syrup

2 tablespoons toasted coconut flakes

2 tablespoons crushed roasted pistachios

2 tablespoons almond butter

1 banana, sliced

⅓ cup raspberries

Acai Bowl

WITH MANGO, KIWIFRUITS, RASPBERRIES, GOJI BERRIES & CHIA SEEDS

The colorful mix of acai berries, raspberries, and goji berries delivers a big dose of antioxidants to this bright-tasting, good-for-you breakfast bowl. If you like, substitute frozen blueberries for the acai berries, dried cranberries for the goji berries, and flaxseeds for the chia seeds.

In a blender, combine the acai, almond milk, bananas, and honey and puree until smooth.

Divide the acai mixture among 4 bowls. Top with the kiwifruits, mango, raspberries, goji berries, and chia seeds. Drizzle with honey, garnish with mint sprigs, and serve.

serves 4

14 oz frozen purée acai, slightly thawed

1 cup almond milk

2 frozen bananas, broken into pieces

2 tablespoons honey, plus more for drizzling

2 kiwifruits, peeled and sliced

1 mango, peeled and cut into chunks

1½ cups raspberries

½ cup goji berries

¼ cup chia seeds

Fresh mint sprigs, for garnish

Feel free to use any type of milk in this recipe, adding more or less to reach the desired consistency.

BASIL-ARUGULA PESTO

1 cup loosely packed arugula
1 cup loosely packed fresh basil leaves
⅓ cup grated Parmesan cheese
¼ cup pine nuts, toasted
1 small clove garlic, minced
½ cup olive oil
Kosher salt and freshly ground pepper

In a food processor, combine the arugula, basil, Parmesan, pine nuts, and garlic and pulse until finely chopped, scraping down the sides of the bowl as needed. With the machine running, add the oil in a steady stream and process until combined. Season with salt and pepper.

makes about 1 cup; serves 4

SUN-DRIED TOMATO PESTO

½ cup drained oil-packed sun-dried tomatoes
5 tablespoons oil from sun-dried tomatoes
2 cloves garlic
¼ cup grated Parmesan cheese
3 tablespoons pine nuts, toasted
½ cup olive oil
Kosher salt and freshly ground pepper

In a food processor, combine the sun-dried tomatoes and their oil, garlic, cheese, and pine nuts and pulse until a thick paste forms. With the machine running, add the olive oil in a steady stream and process until the mixture is cohesive but still slightly chunky. Season with salt and pepper.

makes about 1¼ cup; serves 4

AVOCADO DRESSING

2 avocados, pitted, peeled, and roughly chopped
Juice of 1 lime
Kosher salt

In a food processor, process the avocados until broken up. Add the lime juice and

½ teaspoon salt and process until combined. With the machine running, add ¼ cup water in a steady stream and process until smooth, adding more water as needed to reach the desired consistency. Use right away, or transfer the dressing to an airtight container and refrigerate for up to 1 day.

makes about 1 cup; serves 4

CILANTRO DRESSING

1 tablespoon minced shallot
1 clove garlic
1 cup fresh cilantro leaves
Juice of 1 lime
2 tablespoons white wine vinegar
1 teaspoon honey
Kosher salt
½ cup canola oil

In a food processor, combine the shallot, garlic, and cilantro and pulse until roughly chopped. Add the lime juice, vinegar, honey, and ½ teaspoon salt and process until combined. With the machine running, add the oil in a steady stream and process until completely incorporated. Adjust the seasoning with salt. Use right away, or transfer the dressing to an airtight container and refrigerate for up to 1 week.

makes about 1 cup; serves 4

GREEN GODDESS DRESSING

½ cup loosely packed fresh
flat-leaf parsley leaves
¼ cup minced fresh chives
1 tablespoon minced fresh tarragon
3 anchovy fillets in olive oil
1 tablespoon fresh lemon juice
1 tablespoon olive oil
1 tablespoon white wine vinegar
Kosher salt and freshly ground pepper
¾ cup crème fraîche

In a food processor, combine the parsley, chives, tarragon, anchovies, lemon juice, oil, vinegar, ½ teaspoon salt, and ¼ teaspoon pepper and pulse until finely chopped, scraping down the sides of the bowl as needed. Transfer to a bowl and fold in the crème fraîche. Adjust the seasoning with salt and pepper. Use right away, or transfer the dressing to an airtight container and refrigerate for up to 1 week.

makes about 1 cup; serves 4

TAPENADE DRESSING

12 pitted kalamata olives in brine
¼ cup brine
¼ cup Greek yogurt
1 teaspoon fresh lemon zest
1 garlic clove
Kosher salt and black pepper
¾ cup extra virgin olive oil

In the bowl of a food processor, combine olives, brine, yogurt, zest, garlic, and salt and pepper to taste. Pulse until thick paste forms, about 10 pulses. With the processor running, slowly add olive oil in a steady stream. Continue processing until smooth.

serves 4

MAPLE GLAZE

3 tablespoons maple syrup
3 tablespoons soy sauce
2 tablespoons Asian fish sauce
1 tablespoon firmly packed light brown sugar
4-inch piece fresh ginger, peeled

In a small saucepan over medium heat, combine the maple syrup, soy sauce, fish sauce, brown sugar, ginger, and 1 tablespoon water and bring to a vigorous simmer, whisking frequently. Reduce the heat to medium-low and simmer until the glaze has thickened slightly and becomes glossy, about 5 minutes. Remove from the heat. If the glaze is too thick, add up to 2 tablespoons more water. Remove and discard the ginger before using.

makes about ½ cup; serves 4

LEMON ZA'ATAR YOGURT

1 cup plain Greek yogurt
Zest of 1 lemon
2 teaspoons za'atar
Kosher salt

In a small bowl, stir together the yogurt, lemon zest, za'atar, and ½ teaspoon salt. Use right away, or transfer the yogurt to an airtight container and refrigerate for up to 3 days.

makes about 1 cup; serves 4

CHIMICHURRI

¼ cup sherry vinegar
1 tablespoon Dijon mustard
3 cloves garlic
1 cup fresh flat-leaf parsley leaves
1 cup fresh cilantro leaves
1 cup fresh mint leaves
¾ cup olive oil
1 teaspoon honey
Kosher salt and freshly ground pepper

In a food processor, combine the vinegar, mustard, and garlic and process until blended. Add the parsley, cilantro, mint, and ¼ cup of the oil and pulse until combined. With the machine running, add the remaining ½ cup oil, the honey, and 1 teaspoon salt in a steady stream and process until completely incorporated. Adjust the seasoning with salt and pepper. Use right away, or transfer the chimichurri to an airtight container and refrigerate for up to 1 week.

makes about 1 cup; serves 4

LIME CREMA

½ cup sour cream
1 teaspoon grated lime zest
1 teaspoon fresh lime juice
Kosher salt and freshly ground pepper

In a small bowl, stir together the sour cream and lime zest and juice. Season with salt and pepper. Use right away, or transfer the crema to an airtight container and refrigerate for up to 3 days.

makes about ½ cup; serves 4

PEANUT SAUCE

2" piece ginger, peeled and grated
2 cloves garlic, grated
½ cup smooth peanut butter
2 tablespoons soy sauce
1 tablespoon lime juice
1 teaspoon brown sugar
½ teaspooon red pepper flakes

In a small bowl, mix together ginger, garlic and peanut butter. Stir in the soy sauce, lime juice, brown sugar and red pepper flakes. Stir in enough water to reach the desired consistency.

makes about 1 cup; serves 4

SPANISH RICE

1 tablespoon canola oil
½ yellow onion, finely diced
1 clove garlic, minced
1 tablespoon tomato paste
1½ cups long-grain white rice, rinsed
1 can (10 oz) diced tomatoes with jalapeño and cilantro
2¾ cups vegetable broth
Kosher salt

In a large saucepan over medium heat, warm the oil. Add the onion and cook, stirring occasionally, until tender, about 5 minutes. Add the garlic and tomato paste and cook, stirring occasionally, until fragrant, about 1 minute. Add the rice and cook, stirring occasionally, until it smells nutty, about 2 minutes. Raise the heat to high, add the tomatoes, broth, and 1 teaspoon salt, and bring to a boil. Reduce the heat to low, cover, and simmer until the rice is just tender, about 15 minutes. Remove from the heat and let stand, covered, for 5 minutes. Fluff the rice with a fork.

serves 4

JASMINE RICE

2 cups jasmine rice
Kosher salt

In a large saucepan over medium-high heat, combine the rice, 4 cups water, and 1 teaspoon salt and bring just to a boil. Reduce the heat to low, cover, and cook until the rice is tender and the liquid has been absorbed, 15–20 minutes. Remove from the heat and let stand, covered, for 5 minutes. Fluff the rice with a fork.

serves 4

COCONUT RICE

2 cups jasmine rice
2 cups coconut milk
Kosher salt

In a large saucepan over medium-high heat, combine the rice, coconut milk, 1¾ cups water, and ¼ teaspoon salt and bring just to a boil. Reduce the heat to low, cover, and cook until the rice is tender and the liquid has been absorbed, 15–20 minutes. Remove from the heat and let stand, covered, for 5 minutes. Fluff the rice with a fork.

serves 4

CUCUMBER SALAD

2 cucumbers, halved lengthwise and thinly sliced into half-moons
1 cup fresh mint leaves, thinly sliced
1 tablespoon chili oil
Juice of 1 lemon
Kosher salt and freshly ground pepper

In a bowl, mix the cucumbers, mint, chili oil, and lemon juice. Season to taste with salt and pepper.

serves 4

CUCUMBER-TOMATO SALAD

2 cucumbers, halved lengthwise and cut into half-moons
½ lb cherry tomatoes, halved
2 tablespoons chopped fresh cilantro
2 tablespoons olive oil
Kosher salt and freshly ground pepper

In a bowl, mix the cucumbers, tomatoes, cilantro, and olive oil. Season to taste with salt and pepper.

serves 4—6

CABBAGE SALAD

1½ cups plain Greek yogurt
Zest of 1½ lemons
2 tablespoons fresh lemon juice
2 tablespoons olive oil
1 tablespoon za'atar
2 teaspoons kosher salt
½ head red cabbage, cored and thinly sliced

In a large bowl, mix the yogurt, lemon zest and juice, oil, za'atar, and salt. Add the cabbage and toss gently to coat evenly.

serves 4

RADISH-ASPARAGUS SALAD

1 bunch radishes, trimmed and thinly sliced
¼ lb asparagus, trimmed and thinly sliced
1 teaspoon grated lemon zest
1 tablespoon fresh lemon juice
1 tablespoon olive oil
Kosher salt and freshly ground pepper

In a bowl, mix the radishes, asparagus, lemon zest and juice, and oil. Season to taste with salt and pepper.

serves 4

KIMCHI-ZUCCHINI SLAW

1 zucchini, julienned
2 green onions, white and pale green parts, thinly sliced
2 teaspoons rice vinegar
1 cup cabbage kimchi, roughly chopped
Kosher salt

In a bowl, stir together the zucchini, green onions, and vinegar. Add the kimchi, toss to combine, and season to taste with salt.

serves 4

ROASTED CARROTS

2 lb carrots, peeled and cut into 2-inch pieces
¼ cup olive oil
2 teaspoons ground cumin
Kosher salt

Preheat the oven to 375°F. In a large bowl, toss together the carrots, olive oil, cumin, and 2 teaspoons salt. Spread in a single layer on a baking sheet and roast until fork-tender and slightly charred, about 20 minutes.

serves 4—6

PICKLED CARROTS

5 carrots (about 10 oz total weight), peeled and julienned
¾ cup white vinegar
2½ tablespoons sugar
Kosher salt

Put the carrots in a heatproof bowl. In a small saucepan over medium-high heat, combine ½ cup water, the vinegar, sugar, and 1¼ teaspoons salt. Bring to a simmer, stirring until the sugar and salt are dissolved. Pour over the carrots, making sure they are completely submerged, and let cool to room temperature. Use right away, or transfer the carrots and their liquid to an airtight container and refrigerate for up to 1 week.

serves 4

CRISPY SHALLOT

1 shallot, thinly sliced
½ cup milk
½ cup all-purpose flour
Kosher salt and freshly ground pepper
Canola oil, for frying

Put the shallot in a bowl and cover with the milk. Let stand for 10 minutes, then drain. In a shallow bowl, stir together the flour and a pinch *each* of salt and pepper. Toss the shallot to coat with the flour mixture, shaking off any excess. In a wide, deep frying pan, pour in oil to a depth of ½ inch and heat until it reaches 350°F on a deep-frying thermometer. Add the shallot and fry until crispy and golden brown, about 2 minutes. Transfer to a paper towel–lined plate and season with salt.

serves 4

CRISPY SPICED CHICKPEAS

2 cans (15 oz each) chickpeas, drained, rinsed, and dried
1½ teaspoons ground cumin
1½ teaspoons smoked paprika
Kosher salt
Pinch of cayenne pepper
¼ cup olive oil

In a large bowl, toss together the chickpeas, cumin, paprika, ¼ teaspoon salt, and the cayenne. In a large saut over medium-high heat, warm the oil. Add the chickpeas and cook, stirring frequently, until crispy and golden, about 10 minutes. Using a slotted spoon, transfer to a paper towel–lined plate.

serves 4

PITA CHIPS

3 pita rounds, each cut into 8 wedges
3 tablespoons olive oil
Kosher salt and freshly ground pepper

Preheat the oven to 375°F. Spread the pita wedges in a single layer on a baking sheet. Drizzle with the oil and season with salt and pepper. Bake until crisp, 10–15 minutes.

serves 4

TOASTED FLATBREAD

2 pieces flatbread

Preheat the oven to 375°F. Place the flatbread on a baking sheet and toast until golden and crisp, about 5 minutes. Let cool, then cut into strips.

serves 4

TORTILLA STRIPS

4 corn tortillas, halved and cut into ½-inch strips

2 teaspoons canola oil

½ teaspoon chili powder

½ teaspoon ground cumin

¼ teaspoon garlic powder

¼ teaspoon kosher salt

Preheat the oven to 425°F. In a bowl, toss together the tortilla strips, oil, chili powder, cumin, garlic powder, and salt. Spread in a single layer on a baking sheet. Bake until crisp, 8–10 minutes, stirring once halfway through.

serves 4

SESAME TOASTS

⅓ cup sesame oil

½ baguette, cut on the bias into 8 long, thin slices

In a large frying pan over medium heat, warm the oil. Add the baguette slices and cook until browned and crispy on both sides, about 1 minute per side. Transfer to a plate.

serves 4

POACHED EGGS

4 large eggs

2 teaspoons white vinegar

1 teaspoon kosher salt

Fill a large nonstick frying pan three-fourths full with water and bring to a simmer over medium heat. Add the vinegar and salt. Crack the eggs into individual cups and gently slide the eggs into the simmering water, spacing them evenly apart. Cook until the whites are set, 2–3 minutes. Using a slotted spoon, transfer the eggs to paper towels to drain.

serves 4

MEDIUM-BOILED EGGS

4 large eggs

Fill a saucepan three-fourths full of water and bring to a boil over high heat. Gently drop the eggs into the water and boil for 7 minutes. Drain the eggs and rinse under cold, running water.

makes 4 servings

FRIED EGGS

Vegetable oil, for brushing

4 large eggs

Heat a griddle or two small frying pans over medium-high heat. Brush with vegetable oil. Crack the eggs well apart onto the griddle, or two at a time into the pans. Cook until the white are set but the yolks are still runny, 2–3 minutes.

serves 4

Index

One Bowl Meals

Conceived and produced by Weldon Owen, Inc.
in collaboration with Williams Sonoma, Inc.
3250 Van Ness Avenue, San Francisco, CA 94109

A WELDON OWEN PRODUCTION
1045 Sansome Street, Suite 100
San Francisco, CA 94111
www.weldonowen.com

WELDON OWEN, INC.
President & Publisher Roger Shaw
SVP, Sales & Marketing Amy Kaneko
Finance & Operations Director Philip Paulick

Associate Publisher Amy Marr
Senior Editor Lisa Atwood
Associate Editor Emma Rudolph

Creative Director Kelly Booth
Art Director Marisa Kwek
Production Director Chris Hemesath
Associate Production Director Michelle Duggan
Imaging Manager Don Hill

Photographer Annabelle Breakey
Food Stylist Jen Straus
Prop Stylist Emma Star Jensen

Printed in the USA
First printed in 2017
10 9 8 7 6 5 4 3 2 1

Library of Congress Cataloging-in-Publication
data is available.

ISBN 13: 978-1-68188-245-1

Weldon Owen is a division of Bonnier Publishing USA

ACKNOWLEDGMENTS

Weldon Owen wishes to thank the following people for their
generous support in producing this book: Emily Ayers, Kris Balloun,
Olivia Caminiti, Paul Davies, Gloria Geller, Jackie Hancock, Amy Hatwig,
Xi Hsu, Alexis Mersel, Elizabeth Parson, Sharon Silva,
Kristen Tate, and Lia Valentino.